A PORTRAIT OF
OBEDIENCE

Book Study

Elizabeth Anne Jones

D1545969

Inspired by the book A Portrait of Obedience

LINDA K. STROHECKER AND
SHERRY WYNNE TUCKER

ISBN 978-1-63814-572-1 (Paperback)
ISBN 978-1-63814-573-8 (Digital)

Covenant Books
11661 Hwy 707
Murrells Inlet, SC 29576
www.covenantbooks.com

Introduction and Purpose
for Book Study

A Portrait of Obedience is a beautiful and compelling story, but it is *also a message.* It is the story of two ordinary individuals whose paths are crossed by one extraordinary individual. It is the story of a relationship that is unexpected and life-changing for the characters involved. But the story would not be as beautiful as it is without the reader paying close attention to a very important conversation: the conversation between God and the main characters. The concept of obeying the voice of God is intertwined throughout this story. There are choices to be made—to obey or not to obey—and the results of these choices are what bring to life the beauty in this story.

There are thoughts that may come to your mind. What is obedience? Isn't it just what we are told to do as children as we follow our parents? Maybe the word *obedience* puts a bad taste in your mouth? It sounds like something you do out of obligation. Is it possible that obedience can actually come from a position of love and trust? What if you are asked to do something that makes no sense to you in the moment? How do you obey what God wants you to do when you do not even have the plan, the details? How do you handle the unknowns? Who is involved in such a story?

The characters in this story are real. In this story, you will meet Linda, Bobby, and George. Although Linda and George will appear to be the main characters, you will also witness the faithful, obedience of Bobby, Linda's husband, as he supports her in this journey, reminding us to never underestimate what is going on behind the scenes in the stories we read. Allow these characters to be our teachers as you walk with them. Will you open your heart to see the portrait of obedience being painted in the pages of this book?

This story is filled with characters you will fall in love with, moments that will make you cry, a journey that will keep you on the edge of your seat, and an ending that will fill your heart with wonder and awe. This story has all the makings of a wonderful and creative tale for a reader who needs a heaping dose of encouragement and a feel-good experience. This should be enough, and for many stories it is.

But the purpose of sharing the story is not just to walk you through emotions and to give you an experience that will leave you once you turn that last page of the book. The purpose of sharing this story is to help an ordinary person meet an extraordinary God, to help you, the reader, take a step toward a relationship that will be life-changing. In the hopes that this does not scare you off, we will say that this book is for anyone and everyone! It is for the seeker and the skeptic. It is for the believer and the nonbeliever. It is for the one searching, the discouraged church attendee and the Christian who simply needs a reminder of how big God is. It is for the person hurt by religion and the person who has never believed that there is a God.

Whatever category you find yourself in, this book is for you. This book study is simply a tool to walk you through the experience that is meant for you. You can do this alone if you want, but processing this story with a group will likely provide a much richer experience. We want you to know that you, the participant in this study, has been prayed for, thought about, and considered along the journey, as a cherished, loved individual and as a friend. The reflection questions are crafted to enhance your understanding of the story and what it means for you. May God bless you in your journey through the pages of *A Portrait of Obedience*.

Chapter 1

New Beginnings

In chapter 1, we begin to learn about Linda. *We learn that there are several things that are precious to her: food, family, and faith!*

She is in the middle of unpacking boxes, preparing a meal for her family, and reflecting on a moment in her life that was filled with *new beginnings, comfort food, and family.*

She is overwhelmed but excited by the process of unpacking boxes, thinking about her children and her husband, and looking forward to living in her new home.

What is your first impression of Linda as you read chapter 1? Is there anything extraordinary about Linda, or would you say she seems like a fairly "normal" or ordinary individual? Is there anything about Linda that you relate to?

_____

_____

_____

_____

_____

Linda was beginning a new chapter of her life.

Think of a moment in your life where you were about to begin a new chapter.

What did this time of your life look like? Use all of your senses. What do you see, hear, and smell? Who was with you? How did you feel? Jot down your thoughts below.

_____

_____

_____

_____

_____

New chapters and beginnings are filled with *hope and excitement*. Settle into Linda's new beginning as you think about your own experiences.

Imagine what could be next for Linda...
Imagine what kind of new beginning could be awaiting you...
Write down your thoughts.

_____

_____

_____

_____

_____

It is typical in our world to feel proud of ourselves when accomplishing things. A good marriage, healthy children, and a brand-new home would certainly be a moment to feel proud.

Who *does Linda thank for the blessings in her life?* _____

_____

"She lifted out each picture, reliving the day in her mind and sending up perhaps the millionth, *'Thanks, God. Bobby is such a gift. I do not know what I did to deserve him.'*"

In this moment, Linda is thanking God for the gift of her husband. She states that she does not know what she did to deserve him. In Linda's mind, the person responsible for giving her the gift of her husband is God. God gives good gifts—even gifts we do not deserve, as Linda reflected. *Can you think of a moment in your life* *when you were given something that you did not deserve? How did you feel? Describe the moment.*

_____

_____

_____

_____

_____

Hold onto that image and feeling throughout the story as you see what happens in Linda's life. No one is deserving, yet we are all given the choice to accept the gifts we are offered. Consider how faith in God could tie into this thought.

As you read chapter 1, did you sense that anything extraordinary was about to happen in Linda's life, or would you say that she was simply experiencing an exciting, but fairly ordinary moment?

Circle: *Ordinary   Extraordinary*

How do you define ordinary and extraordinary? Write down an example of each from your own life:

Definition of ordinary: _____

_____

My ordinary moments:_____

_____

Definition of extraordinary: _____

_____

My extraordinary moments: _____

_____

"*That is what the Scriptures mean when they say, 'No eye has seen, no ear has heard, and no mind has imagined what God has pre-*

pared for those who love him'" (1 Corinthians 2:9, NIV).

"Whatever is good and perfect is a gift coming down to us from God our Father" (James 1:17a, NLT).

Whether you are familiar with the Bible or not, whether you believe in God or not, **in reading these Scriptures, what comes to your mind?**

_____

_____

_____

_____

_____

How would you feel knowing that there was a supreme and perfect being who has prepared something special for you, for your life, to teach you and to bless you? When something good happens in your life, do you see it as a gift from God? Why or why not?

_____

_____

_____

_____

_____

Perhaps this book, could be part of a new beginning for you...
As you read the book, you will see that Linda's faith is intertwined throughout each and every moment of her story. You will see Bobby acting in faith as he supports Linda, shows love toward George, and allows God to use his family for a very important calling.
Whatever you may believe, we will challenge you to begin this book as a detective, *looking for treasures of faith.* **May you open your eyes and ears to hear a message from God.**

Guided prayer for those who are searching and seeking:

I do not know who I am praying to. I do not know what You have for me to learn. If You are real, make yourself known to me. If there is a God, I want to know more. I do not understand so many things. Help me to walk this journey with You as I read this story. Help me to know who You are.

Amen.

Guided prayer for the believer:

Lord God, I love You and know that You have plans for me that I cannot even imagine. Sometimes I feel like my life is so ordinary and I want it to be more. I want to live a life that brings You glory, and I want to have eyes that can see and ears that can hear your plans for my life. Help me to grow in my understanding of Your love for me as I read this book.

In Jesus's name. Amen.

Chapters 2–5

The Power of a Moment

Merriam-Webster defines moments as an "*indefinitely short period of time.*"

Some definitions go as far as to say that a moment in "modern seconds" corresponds to approximately ninety seconds. Ninety seconds of time!

A typical day is twenty-four hours, and with this definition in mind, how many moments do we have in each day? Mathematics says that there are approximately forty moments by this definition *in an hour—that is 960 moments in a day!*

Do we pay attention to all 960 of those moments?

Which moments stand out to us the most?

How many moments are simply a blur?

And how many moments stick to us like superglue in the depths of our souls?

Write down your thoughts:

_____

_____

_____

_____

_____

In chapter 2, Linda recalls moments from her life. *What moments stand out to you? How would you describe these moments? How do you think Linda was feeling during this time of her life?*

_____

_____

_____

_____

_____

In particular, **in chapter 3,** there is a very special moment that Linda pays attention to.

It says, *"As Linda unwrapped the last wedding picture in the box,* **she blinked away a tear.** *The photo showed her and her father looking into each other's eyes, snapped by the photographer only a moment before he walked her to the front of the church. She loved this picture of them because* **her father's love for her was captured in a split second."**

Out of all the pictures that Linda looked through, *this moment caused her to tear up.*

There is something about the love and care of a father.

Maybe you have had an experience similar to Linda's, or maybe you have had nothing but heartache and disappointment when it comes to your relationship with your father.

Did you know that you have a Father in heaven?

Psalm 103:13 says, "The Lord is like a father to his children, tender and compassionate to those who fear him."

This moment in Linda's life was so impactful that it caused her to cry.

There was something special, powerful, and genuine in that look captured by the photographer.

If someone were to capture a picture of you and your father or father figure, what would that look like to you?

_____

_____

_____

_____

_____

It is entirely possible that even thinking of such a picture can cause heartache, sadness, or regret. There could possibly be feelings of resentment and anger. We certainly all have not had the wonderful love of a kind and generous father.

What would it look like to have a father that is described in the Bible verse above?

Psalm 103:13 says, "The Lord is like a father to his children, tender and compassionate to those who fear him."

How does **Psalm 103:13** describe God as father? What two words are used to describe him?

_____ and _____

*How different would your life be **if you knew that God was tender and compassionate toward you?** How different would your life be if you knew that you had a father in heaven who would meet all of your deepest needs as a father? What would that snapshot look like?*

Meditate on this moment in time that Linda experienced.

Think about your own experiences with your own father.

Consider what it would be like to have a tender and compassionate God.

Write down your thoughts:

_____

_____

_____

_____

_____

There is another moment in which Linda ponders on Bobby, *this man who would become our behind-the-scenes hero in this story.*

Linda's father is concerned about Bobby before they marry because Linda and Bobby have not known each other for very long. In time, her father begins to see that Bobby is *"genuine to a fault and full of heart, as he loved, honored, and cherished his new bride."*

Bobby's character is so important in this story and it will be crystal clear that God uses Bobby in such pivotal moments to help encourage Linda. Obedience takes many shapes and forms. We will see that Bobby's obedience is the *anchor* to Linda's.

It will be clear that Bobby's obedience to God is nothing short of amazing.

Lastly, there is another key moment in **chapter 4** where Linda goes for a walk. She wanted a chance to relax and unwind, and her way of relaxing and connecting with the Lord was taking a walk. This was simply a normal part, a normal rhythm of her day.

What happened to Linda while she was on her walk? Who did she meet? What kind of impression did this person leave on her? _____

_____

_____

_____

_____

How would you describe George? Do you relate to George in any way?

_____

_____

_____

_____

_____

It is apparent in this new character that George is going to have an impact on Linda's life. She even said a prayer for him: *"Lord, please take care of George. I do not know him, but he is on my heart. He is your child, and he matters. Let him know you're there and that you care for him."*

This was a moment in time that could have not even occurred.

In this day and age, we are all, busy, isolated, and maybe even just used to withdrawing from people. Sometimes we do not even say hi to people when we enter a store, get onto elevators, or walk our neighborhoods. Sometimes we purposely ignore our neighbors, rush to our cars as we leave our home to go to work and when we get home, rush back inside. We can certainly feel awkward around strangers.

George seemed to have an unusual life circumstance, and it would be easy for Linda to walk by because she felt uncomfortable or intrusive.

It might have even felt more comfortable to simply leave him alone.

Compare the two moments: **Linda's photograph with her father and meeting George.**

*Would you say these moments are **equal in value?***
Circle: *Yes   No*

Why did you choose your answer? _____
_____
_____
_____
_____

*How can we decide which moments are important or not?*_____
_____
_____
_____
_____

Could there possibly be a bigger story we are not aware of? Can you recall a moment in your life that seemed insignificant at the time but turned out to be life-changing later on?
Write down your thoughts. _____
_____
_____
_____
_____

Guided prayer for those who are searching and seeking:

I pray that I would open my eyes to the moments in my life that are important. I am not sure if I believe that You are a part of the moments in my life, but if You are here, help me to know that. Help me to know You as my Father, loving and compassionate.

Help me to picture Your loving face and understand more of who You are. Help me to see the people in my life through Your eyes.

Help me to look for opportunities to get to know people that I would not normally seek out in the past. Help me to remember that everyone carries a burden and help me to be sensitive to that. Amen.

Guided prayer for the believer:

Lord, help me to see Your heart as I read this story. Help me to understand the importance of the people You place in my life. Help me to take time to notice people and to not take for granted opportunities that I have to simply connect with another human being.

Lord, help me to remember that everyone has a story, and everyone carries around hurt and need. Use me to share Your love with people in my life. Help me to understand the power of a moment. In Jesus's name. Amen.

Chapter 5

George

How old was George when he started coming to his parent's cottage to take care of it? _____

How old was George now? _____

What do you think kept George coming back to this place? What do you think it meant for him to spend time at this place, even if it were just to simply rake the leaves in the front yard?

_____
_____
_____
_____
_____

What were the circumstances surrounding George's childhood? Describe his father and his relationship with George? _____

_____
_____
_____
_____

What happened in the following years?
1911: _____ **1950:** _____ **1990:** _____

How would you feel if you were George? Would you continue to come back to a place filled with difficult and sad memories? _____
_____

What were some good memories that George had of his childhood?
_____
_____

What haunted George as a child? _____
_____

What role did art and creativity play in George's life? _____
_____

In **chapter 5**, it says that George built a lifelong career with the *Star* and the *Washington Post*.

It says that he even opened an art studio. George was clearly very talented!

Would your first impression of George as described by Linda be of someone who owned an art studio and built a career with well-known newspapers?
Circle: Yes No

Do you think knowing George's vocation and status in his past would have changed Linda's desire to know him?
Circle: Yes No

George states that after his retirement he continued to draw and that his art was *"the only remedy for purging his soul in its entirety and breathing life into that which had no other alternative than to exist."*

Why do you think George needed a remedy for his soul? How did art help him cope with his life?

_____

_____

_____

_____

_____

Once again, think about his character. Now that you know more about him, is there anything about George's character that you can relate to? Write down your thoughts.

_____

_____

In this moment, George's world collided with Linda's.

When Linda stopped to talk to George, her conversation appeared to be very simple and innocent, a neighbor simply asking another neighbor to stop by anytime, to come over if there was anything he ever needed. *Yet this encounter, this simple moment, seemed to have an impact on both of them.*

Chapter 6–9

Living Faith: George, Bobby, and Linda

In **chapters 6 and 7**, Linda's relationship with George takes a dramatic change.

How would you describe her relationship with George at the beginning of **chapter 6***?*

_____

_____

Who is the first person to see that George is in need?
Circle: Linda   Bobby

Who calls 911?
Circle: Linda   Bobby

This is an important detail as, once again, we see how Bobby's role is foundational to Linda's ability to minister to George's needs.

Linda invited George to come over any time when she first met him.

What do you think would have happened if Linda had not stopped by to talk with George and introduce herself? What would he have done when he began to have his heart attack?

_____

_____

When George first meets Linda, he has a flashback.

He thinks about a woman who was once a part of his life.

In **chapter 5**, after Linda walks away from him, it says, "She left a void in his heart, his life. Then this neighbor, Linda, looking so much like her with grace and light spilling out of her like so many stars, was standing in front of him half a lifetime later. The resemblance was uncanny on so many levels."

Do you believe in coincidences? Some people do. Some people believe that things happen for a reason, and some people believe things do not happen for any reason other than mere chance.

Do you think that George would have gone to Linda's house if she had not reminded him of someone so dear to him from his past?
Circle: No   Maybe   Yes

Write down why you chose your answer: _____
_____
_____
_____
_____

Linda's prayer:

"Father, please let George be okay. Give him a sense of peace. He must be so scared right now. I know I am. Give me whatever I need, to do whatever it is you need me to do to help George. Please guide the paramedics and doctors' hands as they help him. I do not know what your plan is here, but thank you for allowing us to meet today. I can't imagine what would have happened if he didn't come here tonight."

Does Linda believe that she has a role to play in George's life at this moment?
Circle: Yes   No

What does she ask God to give her during this moment? _____
_____
_____

What does she ask God to give George at this moment? _____

_____

_____

Fate and destiny are thought to be courses of events that are *beyond human control.* Many people say they believe in fate or destiny but not necessarily a supreme being or God.

If Linda and George had not met (could be by fate, destiny, or maybe through God's plan), it is possible that George would have died.

In reflecting on Linda's prayer, *who does Linda believe is in control of what is happening in her and George's life at this moment? Who is she trusting in?* _____.

Christians often quote **Psalm 139** in reflecting on God being in control of one's life, *even before birth.*

Psalm 139:13 (NIV) says, "For you created my inmost being, you knit me together in my mother's womb."

Psalm 139:16 (ESV) says, "Your eyes saw my unformed substance; in your book were written, every one of them, the days that were formed for me, when as yet there was none of them."

What do you think about these passages of Scripture? Do you think they could be true? How would you feel about a God who knew you and formed you even in your mother's womb?

_____

_____

_____

_____

_____

Linda responds to George's condition by immediately assessing his physical appearance and taking action by having Bobby call 911. George looks to Linda and she sees *pleading in his eyes. What does she offer to do?* _____

_____

John 15:13 (NIV) says, "Greater love has no one than this: to lay down one's life for one's friends."

1 John 4:16 says, "And so we know and rely on the love God has for us. God is love. Whoever lives in love lives in God, and God in them."

What do these verses in the Bible say about love? Who do they say, "is love"?

_____
_____
_____
_____
_____

Do you think this is the kind of love that Linda has in her heart? How do you know?

_____
_____
_____
_____
_____

In reviewing **chapter 7**, we see that Linda goes to the hospital with George. There is a nurse who asks Linda why she did what she did. *How does Linda respond?*

_____
_____
_____
_____
_____

How would you describe Linda's relationship with George at the end of **chapter 7**? _____

_____

At the end of a very long day, who is waiting for Linda in the waiting room? _____

_____

"Side by side with their strides in perfect lock step, they walked out of the emergency room doors into the night air. Their hands joined as they made their way to the car."

What would it mean to Linda to have Bobby waiting for her after such a traumatic experience? _____

_____

Linda goes home that night with Bobby. It had been a very long day filled with something she certainly did not expect when she woke up that morning.

Think about how she must have felt when she went to sleep that night.

Think about how you would feel after having a similar day.

What does it mean to live out your faith? Live what you believe? Linda and Bobby lived out their faith. Do you live out yours? Think about these things as you pray…

Guided prayer for those who are searching and seeking:

Help me to understand more about You. Help me to understand why Linda responded to George the way that she did. Could it be that you are in control of all things? Could it be that You knew me from the beginning of time? Help me to understand who You are in my life? I do not know what I believe in. I want to live a life that is good. Teach me how.

Guided prayer for the believer:

Thank You for knitting me together in my mother's womb. Thank You for being in control of all things. Help me to have such a close relationship with You that I am willing and ready to do anything you ask of me at any moment in time. Help me to be ready for whatever You have for me. Give me the kind of love for people that You gave Linda for George.

Chapter 10

Family, Home, and Roots

In **chapter 10**, we learn about Linda's family. Family is very import-ant. The way that we grow up and the people we spend our time with in those early years through young adulthood truly do shape and form who we are. *How would you describe the family you grew up in?*

_____

_____

_____

_____

_____

What are some things that you learned from your family that are still important to you today?

_____

_____

_____

_____

*How would you describe Linda's extended family? Who were the family members that she spoke of in **chapter 10**? What was their life like? What kind of impact did her family have on the people whom they welcomed into their home?*

_____

_____

_____

_____

_____

Linda talks about several different kinds of people her family reached out to over the years—*the homeless man struggling with alcohol, a cousin who grew up right alongside Linda and her family, Linda's uncle who had polio, her cousin's mother who was a nurse, a family transitioning between homes, a large family whose father was in between jobs, and a "broken" woman.*

What did all of these people have in common? Simply stated, they needed a place to call home for a season or period of time in their life. They needed a place to find rest, comfort, food, stability, healing.

How would you describe the perfect home?

_____

_____

_____

_____

_____

When people came to Linda's family's homes, their needs were met.

Linda learned from these stories and from what she witnessed that people even left their home *better, restored, rested.*

She learned that sometimes just simply being there for someone can be enough and that simple acts of kindness are long-lasting and truly meaningful. Certainly, what Linda and her family provided for others is wonderful. They met the needs of the people who came to their home.

Philippians 4:19 says, "And my God will meet all your needs according to the riches of his glory in Christ Jesus."

What does Philippians 4:19 say about the needs that God will meet? What needs does God meet?

Circle: some needs   most needs   all needs

Linda talked about her grandparents' home being modest and even the home that she grew up in being small, but warm and loving. Having an abundance of things and space did not influence what Linda's family did with their home.

It was always a place of welcome.

It is truly amazing to think of a family willing to give so much to others out of what could even be considered poverty, compared to the modern world that we live in.

To give out of abundance is one thing, but to give out of scarcity is another.

When people left Linda's family's homes, do you think they would remember only the physical things such as the food, clothing, bed to sleep in, roof over their head?

Would there be something more they would remember? Write down what non-physical things they may remember…

_____

_____

_____

_____

_____

What are your greatest needs right now in this season of life?

_____

_____

_____

_____

Fill in the blank...
**"And, my God, will meet all your needs, according to _____
_____ of his glory in Christ Jesus" (Philippians 4:19).**

What does the riches of His glory in Christ Jesus mean to you? If you are not sure, make a guess. Are these riches as in wealth, money, things, property, treasure? Is this richness referring to something else? Something deeper? Do you personally know what these riches are?

_____

_____

_____

_____

_____

Let us look at another piece of Scripture.
Ephesians 3:14–17 *says, "For this reason I kneel before the Father, from whom every family in heaven and on earth derives its name. I pray that out of his glorious riches he may strengthen you with power through his Spirit in your inner being, so that Christ may dwell in your hearts through faith."*

This passage is a prayer from the apostle Paul who was a missionary—someone who traveled to tell others about Jesus. He ministered to a church in a place called Ephesus (hence the name of the book of the bible, Ephesians). *What does he pray for?*

The church to be _____.
With power from who? _____
So that WHO can dwell in the hearts of the people? _____

_____

He prays for strength for the church that will come out of "his glorious riches."

A home is a dwelling place. Linda's home was a place for many who needed somewhere to dwell in safety. The Bible talks about our hearts being a home, a place for Jesus to dwell.

What do you think about this? Is your heart a place where Jesus would be welcomed? Why or not? _____

_____

_____

_____

_____

Guided prayer for those who are searching and seeking:

Linda had a family that developed strong roots for her. She was able to give and love others because of what she had witnessed. Help me to learn what it means to serve and to share my life with other people. Help me to see the needs of people around me. Help me to understand my own needs. Help me to be a part of making someone else's life better. Help me to understand how You might be a part of meeting my own needs.

Guided prayer for the believer:

Lord Jesus, I know that according to the riches of Your grace You will meet all of my needs. Help me to put my trust in You. As You meet my needs, help me to realize that You have given me more than enough to share with others in need. Help me to see the people in my life who need a family, a home, a place to be welcomed. And help me to be willing to be used by You.

Chapters 11–13

Not Forsaken

In **chapter 11**, Linda calls Bobby to tell him that she would be coming home with "George in tow." Most husbands would perhaps not be thrilled to have their wives bringing home a sick, elderly man, who claims to have no family. *What does Bobby do to show kindness to George?*

_____

_____

A simple act of kindness can go a long way. Think about how long it may have been since George's old car had been treated to a wash. This is another example of Linda and George's "behind-the-scenes hero."

Linda says goodbye to George after picking him up from the hospital following his heart attack. Linda drives him back from the hospital in hopes of getting him back to what he hoped would be a "normal life."

Linda continues to try to understand George's situation. She asks him if he has any family to help him out, a question she has asked several times before. George continues to give her the same answer: **He has no one**.

If you put yourself in George's shoes, how would you feel at this moment in time? Picture yourself leaving the hospital, you have just had a heart attack, probably one of the scariest things that has ever happened to you. The one person who has reached out to you is still a stranger, but someone who cares, and you are having to say goodbye. *You are leaving to go back to the life you once knew, alone and without family or anyone to help.*

Write down your thoughts:

_____

_____

_____

_____

_____

It is **2002**—six years since George's heart attack. It has been six years since Linda had gone for that walk and met George as he raked leaves next door at the cottage that his parents raised him in. Linda had kept in touch but had not seen George other than passing him by if she saw him at the cottage.

Linda's life had continued on. She was still busy with work and her family had grown.

She continued to be thankful for all that God had given her.

She receives a phone call from Bobby that once again, George was in need of help.

Once again, Bobby is the one to find George in need and make the first step.

Linda prayed: *"Father, please let everything be okay. My heart is afraid, but I know that You are in control here. Please keep my head clear and allow me to help George through whatever is going on. My trust is in You, Lord, not in what I see.*

*In this prayer, Linda expresses her feelings—**she is afraid**.*

*In this prayer, Linda expresses her faith, **she knows that God is in control**.*

*In this prayer, Linda asks for her next step to **continue to be there for George**.*

*In this prayer, Linda indicates that **her trust is not in what she sees in front of her, but in the Lord**.*

Have you ever prayed a prayer like this? **Circle**: Yes No

How would you describe Linda's relationship with God just by reading this prayer?
Circle: Distant Good Close Very Close

Why did you choose your answer?

_____

_____

_____

_____

_____

In **chapter 12**, *Linda notices some things about George that concern her; what are those things?*

_____

_____

_____

_____

_____

Based on what she sees, it is likely that *George has been alone for a long time and not taking care of himself.* Once again, Linda finds herself responding to another health crisis and gets him to the hospital.

George says he was *"trying to get to her."*

Again, we can assume that if he did not get to her, it is possible that he could have lost his life (this would be the second time)!

He knew he was ill, and he was drawn back to Linda, still somewhat of a stranger and not a close family member or friend.

Linda takes George to the hospital and leaves him once again to recover.

George thinks again about Peta, the woman from his past whom he loved so dearly and how much of a resemblance Linda is to her.

George was most definitely a man who felt emotions deeply.

For someone like George, not having anyone to care for him must have been devastating. To have someone come into his life who resembles the one person he cared so deeply for in his life, must have been astounding to him, certainly stirring up emotions.

The last sentence in chapter 13 says, *"What an incredible gift, this late in his life, to be able to look past the pain and once again see the beauty. Such comfort to know he had not been forsaken."*

How would you define the word forsaken? _____

_____

In Deuteronomy 31:6, it says: *"Be strong and courageous. Do not be afraid or terrified because of them, for the LORD your God goes with you; he will never leave you nor forsake you."*

Deuteronomy 31:6 was written to encourage the people of Israel, including Joshua, Solomon, and Hezekiah's military officers. Their Old Testament reality presented their lives with insurmountable challenges, and *God wanted them to know unequivocally that they could trust Him to lead them to victory.*

It was a call to obedience amid great adversity.

Two verses later God repeated, *"The Lord himself goes before you and will be with you; he will never leave you nor forsake you. Do not be afraid; do not be discouraged"* (Deuteronomy 31:8).

When *we* promise "always" or "never," we are not necessarily always capable of upholding it.

However, when God promises "always" or "never," He can be fully trusted to honor His word.

If you knew that you had a God who would never forsake you, how would you react to Him?

_____

_____

_____

_____

_____

Think about George, think about Linda, think about how their lives have been intertwined and how close to death George came... *twice* now.

If it is hard to picture God for yourself, think about this story and what it would mean to George to have someone there for him after feeling forsaken, especially after losing the woman he loved so much, being alone for years, most likely depressed and obviously declining in his health.

Most likely, at some point in our lives, we can relate to George. We have been there. We have experienced loss, loneliness, depression, and more.

But George was not forgotten! He was not forsaken!

His life was orchestrated in such a way that he had met someone that would help him in the most difficult times. George was blessed! He was not forsaken.

Have you ever felt forgotten? Like no one can really see you? I think we all have.

Guided prayer for those who are searching and seeking:

There are times in my life where I have felt forsaken and forgotten. I do not like to think about these times because they were very painful. I would like to believe that there is someone who cares about me all the time, 100 percent, no holding back. Someone who will always be there for me. If that is You, please reveal Yourself to me. Help me to not feel forsaken in my life.

Guided prayer for the believer:

Lord God, I know that You are here, I trust in Your word, and You have provided for me in my life in many ways. Help me to be overwhelmed with worship and awe as I think about this story that I am reading about Linda and George. If I have lost my passion for You and the joy in knowing how faithful You are, please renew it in this moment! Help me to remember that You will never leave me nor forsake me.

Chapter 14

A Servant's Heart

Linda goes to visit George in the hospital. *What does she notice about his feet?* She notices that they are infected! She notices that his toenails are long and, with her background in podiatry, she knows when she has seen bad feet.

What does Linda do for George? _____

_____

Is this something that you would have done if you were in her shoes?
Circle: Absolutely Not!   Maybe   Yes!

Why did you pick your answer? _____

_____

_____

_____

_____

How do you think this act made George feel? _____

_____

Linda thought about a story in the Bible while she was doing this.

John 13:3–5 says:

> **Jesus knew that the Father had put all things under his power, and that he had come from God and was returning to God; so, he got up from the meal, took off his outer clothing, and wrapped a towel around his waist. After that, he poured water into a basin and began to wash his disciples' feet, drying them with the towel that was wrapped around him.**

Jesus demonstrated *humility and care*. He also *had a message to send*. The message was that his disciples needed to be clean, not of the dirt on their feet, *but of the dirt in their hearts*.

This simple act was to show that unless they be washed away of their sins, they cannot inherit the kingdom of God.

The message of repentance and forgiveness was at the very heart of Christ's teachings.

Washing someone's feet is a very intimate thing to do. It is very possible that the disciples would have been embarrassed by what Jesus was doing.

It is possible that George would have been embarrassed at what Linda was doing.

The reason the disciples were not embarrassed is because *they knew Jesus's love for them. Linda was demonstrating the love of Jesus to George by washing his feet.*

Feel free to explore this story more. If you have a Bible, look up and read more of John, chapter 13. If you do not have a Bible, download one on your phone. Talk to a friend about what you find out. Write down your thoughts below:

_____

_____

_____

_____

_____

Write down your own prayer this time as you think about these events...

_____

_____

_____

_____

_____

Chapters 15–20

A New Family

In chapter 15, George is *told that he will have to live in a rehabilitation center until he is stronger and then possibly move into assisted living.*

At this time, Linda still does not know what her role is, *but she keeps showing up.*

Linda really begins to wonder what her role is in George's life. On page 64, she is drinking some hot chocolate from the vending machine at the hospital and thinks to herself, "Wait. I'm not his caretaker, am I?"

Have you ever been in a situation where you felt like you were "in too deep"?

Linda buys him new clothes and helps him prepare for the rehabilitation center. She notices that George is scared and nervous. He is not going home. This time the damage to his heart is too much and he needs daily assistance.

How does Linda feel about George going to the rehabilitation facility? _____

Who does Linda turn to for support as she processes this next step for George? _____

Linda discovers that the rehabilitation center that George is in is not taking good care of him, and in fact the conditions and treatment are neglectful. At this point, Linda decides that she cannot sit back and leave him there.

*What does Linda decide to do?*_____

_____

*How does this one decision change everything for her role in George's life?*_____

_____

When Linda brings George home, as you can imagine, there are a lot of emotions—hers, George's, Bobby's.

Linda is nervous about what she has gotten herself into, she wonders how will she care for George? What will this mean for her life? George is relieved to have Linda and a place to stay.

*Bobby has a supportive response. What does he say on page 72?*___

_____

_____

At the end of **chapter 16**, George is now staying at her home. She has purchased prescriptions for him, bought him clothing and personal items, and given him dinner and a place to lay his head.

Now this story is starting to sound familiar. *This is exactly the kind of thing her family has always done, but understandably, Linda is unsure of herself as this is a really big step to take.*

This is when her obedience to what God has called her to do begins to really impact her life, her family, everything that she knows.

This is when obedience starts to look like sacrifice and risk.

What are your thoughts on what Linda did? Do you think she could have made these decisions without Bobby's support? Without her faith?

_____

_____

_____

_____

_____

As Linda begins to care for George, she realizes that it is almost like she has adopted a new baby! She recognizes how much he needs and how much work it will be to take care of him. She continues to struggle with what to do next.

During this time, George and Linda share simple moments together, having breakfast, sitting outside and looking at the water, introducing George to the family dog, and getting to know each other. Linda begins to ask George questions. She begins to learn his story. Let us see if we know his story by now…

*How old was George when his parents bought the cottage?*_____
_____

*How was George involved with building the cottage?*_____
_____

What was George's favorite thing to do when he was at the cottage?
_____
_____

George recalls the time when his father fell. This moment in his life is very significant.
What was George's father's profession? _____
_____

Where did he work when he fell? _____
_____

How old was George when his father fell? _____
_____

Linda says that the guilt was evident on George's face as he spoke about this.

What did George believe about his father's paralysis? _____
_____

Do you think this burden and this sense of responsibility impacted George's life? How?

_____

_____

_____

_____

_____

How might sharing this story with Linda, open a door for Linda to see more deeply into George's life? His pain? _____

_____

_____

_____

_____

In chapters 19 and 20, Linda begins to hear a message. She begins to put the pieces together on how to continue obeying God, by caring for George, while also living her life.

*What plan does she come up with?*_____

_____

_____

_____

_____

*What is Bobby's reaction to this plan? What does his reaction tell you about Bobby's heart?*_____

_____

_____

_____

_____

How does trusting in God relate to this plan as you review the Scripture verses Linda focuses on in pages 84 and 85. *Paraphrase these* *verses in your own words. Be creative! Write this out in a way that makes sense to you: **Proverbs 16:9, 19:21, 3:5–6.***

_____

_____

_____

_____

_____

_____

_____

_____

_____

_____

Finish this section off by naming some things. Naming is a powerful process.

Name the main characters in this story: _____

_____

Name the struggles that George has faced in his life: _____

_____

Name the ways in which Linda and Bobby have been obedient to what God has asked them to do:_____

_____

_____

_____

_____

Lastly, name your feelings about God as you have considered Him through the eyes of this story; as you enter into the middle of this amazing story, where do you find your own thoughts going? _____

_____

_____

_____

Chapter 21

Redemption

The cottage was a very special place for George. *What kinds of memories does he have of growing up there?* _____
_____
_____
_____
_____

    The cottage had worn down over the years, just like George had. He tried to do something to keep it up, to show it care. What that looked like was simply raking leaves. It was what he could do, and he was faithful to doing it when he could.

    But George could no longer take care of the cottage or himself. He tried, but his efforts were not enough.

    His cottage was in need of restoration, and in many ways, so was George.

    You could even say that the cottage represented George—filled with memories, aching for care, lonely for company, lost without someone to bring it back to life.

What might it mean to George to have the opportunity to see his cottage rebuilt, recreated, to see new life come back into this place that was so dear to his heart?

_____

_____

_____

_____

_____

George's cottage was in need of restoration and renovation...

Another word that comes to mind is **redemption**. George's cottage and his life were experiencing a kind of redemption.

Webster's defines redemption as the following:

Circle which definition you feel connects best with what was happening to the cottage. How about to George?

the act of making something better or more acceptable.

to change for the better

to make worthwhile

to make good

the act of correcting a past wrong

to atone for

to help to overcome something detrimental.

to free from what distresses or harms

to offset the bad effect of

Explain your answers here:

_____

_____

_____

_____

In the Bible, redemption *refers to the deliverance of sinners from their sin, leading to salvation.* Redemption is used to refer *both to deliverance from sin and to freedom from captivity.*

Is there anything in George's life that has held him captive? What does George need deliverance from? _____

_____

_____

_____

_____

Is there anything in your life that has held you captive? Is there anything in your life that has been worn down from years of neglect? Something you have tried to tend to, but you just cannot seem to fix? To redeem?

What would your life look like if you had redemption? Are you still raking leaves, hoping to bring back what once was? How would you like to see your life be renewed and restored?

Think about this. Write down any thoughts...

_____

_____

_____

_____

_____

In Christian theology, *Jesus is referred to as the Redeemer.*
Romans 3:23 says, *"for all have sinned and fall short of the glory of God..."*
Anyone who is a slave needs to be redeemed or bought back. There is a ransom to be paid. *Jesus Christ pays the price for sin by dying on a cross and offers freedom for those who believe in Him.*
Galatians 5:1 says, *"it is for freedom that Christ has set you free."*
What might it meant to you to live in freedom?
Think about this as you continue to read about George, Linda, Bobby, the cottage and as you reflect on your own life.

Chapter 22

Connection and Trust

*In **chapter 22**, when Linda is going to work after being home with George, how is she feeling?*

_____
_____
_____
_____
_____

Who is staying with George while she goes to work? _____
_____

What do you notice about the connections that George makes with Linda's parents? It would be easy to think that Linda's parents are doing Linda and George a favor by being there with George. How would this time be a blessing also for Linda's parents?

_____
_____
_____
_____
_____

Name all the ways that God provided for Linda and George during this day.

_____

_____

_____

_____

_____

How does Linda explain why worrying can be prideful? Do you agree with her? Explain your answer. _____

_____

_____

_____

_____

In thinking about our behind-the-scenes hero, Bobby, how does he come through at the end of this wonderful day to help George move back into his cottage?

_____

_____

_____

_____

Based on what happened during this day, in just looking at this snapshot in time, do you think that God showed himself to be trustworthy?
Circle: Yes   No

Name the characteristics of what you think a trustworthy God would be like:_____

_____

_____

_____

_____

How would you feel about following a trustworthy God? When you think about how He provided for Linda's family and for George in just one simple day, how do you feel about Him? Think about this and in your heart, quietly talk to God about your feelings and thoughts.

Chapter 23–24

Obedience and Sacrifice

In chapter 23, the reality of being a 24-7 caretaker starts to sink in for Linda. Her husband wants to go away for the weekend with her and she realizes that she cannot go. Linda struggles with several emotions and thoughts during this time.

What do you notice that is difficult for her about this experience?

_____

_____

_____

_____

_____

Linda has an interesting experience after watching Bobby pull out of the driveway and crying out to God. *What does she hear? What message does God give her? Write it out below.*

_____

_____

_____

_____

_____

Linda realizes that this voice must be from the Lord. After she hears from him in her heart, she is able to move on and enjoy the weekend despite feeling left out and struggling with her responsibilities.

Do you think that in Linda's heart, the sacrifices she is making are worth it? Do you think at this point she would like to turn back and change the decisions that she has made? Explain your answer below:

_____
_____
_____
_____
_____

Linda continues to process what she heard from God and asked herself two questions. Write down the questions below:

_____
_____
_____
_____
_____

What is the answer that she comes up with to her questions?

_____
_____
_____
_____
_____

Fill in the blanks to complete **Ephesians 2:8–9** below:
"For it is by _____ that you have been _____, through _____—and it is not from _____, it is the _____ of _____—not by _____, so that no one can boast."

Linda says that it was only her choice to be obedient to God that prompted her to blindly help George. She is insinuating that she may not have made this decision if God had not kept her from thinking about the sacrifices that would have to be made.

In the end, she says only one thing is important.

She says there was only one real choice that she had to make.

What was that choice? To be _____ *or to be* _____.

Although Linda missed out on a beautiful weekend with her husband and maybe missed out on making memories with him, there was something special about the time she spent with George. *What special memory did they make together toward the end of the chapter?*

_____

_____

_____

_____

_____

What sacrifices do both Linda and Bobby make in order to welcome George into their life in this chapter?

_____

_____

_____

_____

_____

Are you willing to make sacrifices to do what is right? Think of a time where you had to make a sacrifice. Was it worth it to you in the end?

_____

_____

_____

_____

_____

Why do you think obeying God was the most important thing to Linda?

_____

_____

_____

_____

_____

Chapters 25

Church

Linda talks in chapter 25 about a sweet moment she has with God where she really ponders and examines herself, her actions and what the Bible says.

What does she call her church experience? _____

If you have had any experience with church, what would you call your experience? _____
_____

Linda prays to God using an acronym. Write down what it stands for below:

A: _____
C: _____
T: _____
S: _____

If you would like to, write out your own ACTS prayer below. Here are some headings to get you started:

A: God I adore you. You are _____
_____ (think of words to describe God).

C: Lord, I confess the following _____
_____ (think of things you regret, things you are sorry for).

T: God, I thank you for _____
_____ (think of things you are thankful for).

S: Lord, please answer my prayers for _____
_____.
(Ask God for what you need.)

It says that she "basked in His love." *What do you think that means?* _____
_____
_____
_____
_____
_____

She talks about light. She quotes **Matthew 5:16**. Fill in the blanks below to write out this verse:

"In the same way, _____ your _____ shine before _____, so that they may _____ _____ _____ _____ and _____ your _____ in _____."

Many times, we do things so that others will notice. When we do something good, it feels good for other people to praise us. In the Bible, followers of Jesus are told to shine the light of Christ not for themselves but so that others can know God.
What do you think the light of Christ means? Is there anything that you see in Linda's life that would reflect the light of Christ based on what you know? _____
_____
_____
_____
_____.

Does Linda think she has to be perfect to shine the light of Christ?
Circle: Yes   No

Does Linda choose to shine the light of Christ, despite her own imperfections?
Circle: *Yes   No*

Do you think she can do this on her own? Or does she need God's help? Think about this.

Does Linda believe that she has to make herself good? _____
_____

If her good works do not save her, what does? _____
_____

Did she care if her choices looked crazy to other people? _____
_____

Chapters 25–28

Treasures and Memories

Linda and George visit his old home. It is a beautiful home, but as Linda walks around with George, she sees the neglect.

"Looking past the beautiful bones, Linda was sad to see evidence of perhaps years of reclusion."

George is emotional as he enters his home and walks around. He is getting ready to sell his home and there is much to let go of, but also there are things to keep.

Letting go and holding on are some of the hardest things in life.

At George's age and considering all he has been through, do you think it would be easy or hard for him to let go of his old home?
Explain below:

_____

_____

_____

_____

_____

There are things in his home that he wants to keep and hold on to. They are listed below:
Why do you think these treasures are special to George?
His mother and father's Bibles: _____

_____

Box of pictures: _____
_____

His mother's small, ornate, mirror: _____
_____

His father's cuff links: _____
_____

His father's stone carvings: _____
_____

What are some things you would keep from your home if you had to move suddenly? What makes these things special to you? _____
_____
_____
_____
_____

These treasures are what George will bring with him.

They will bring him joy, good memories, and help him stay connected to his past.

These things are special indeed, but they are not the ultimate treasure in George's life, nor are "things" ever the most important treasure in any of our lives.

In **2 Corinthians 4:7**, it says, ***"But we have this treasure in jars of clay to show that this all-surpassing power is from God and not from us."***

Clay jars were containers created by skilled potters who took raw clay, shaped and molded it as they desired, and then baked the clay until it was hard. The jars were painted, glazed, or decorated for whatever purpose they had in mind. In ancient times, sacred scrolls or valuable documents were rolled up and placed inside a jar of clay and then hidden for safekeeping.

One thing they had in common was that they were breakable.

Contents could not be forever housed in jars of clay.

Clay jars were temporary holding places. This verse in the Bible indicates that we are like "jars of clay" with a "treasure" inside.

Our physical bodies are like those jars and are temporary housing places for the treasure God has given us, namely, *"the light of the gospel that displays the glory of Christ"* (2 Corinthians 4:4). **The knowledge of the gospel is the treasure.**

What do you think about this? _____
_____
_____
_____
_____

When George allowed Linda to enter his home, this was another step in their relationship. George was a private person and oftentimes focused on his art and the rhythm of his work life as he lived on his own. It is unlikely that George had dinner parties, friends stopping by on occasion or holiday celebrations.

"This nearly broken Linda's heart. She swallowed hard, taking a breath to steady her emotions."

As Linda enters his home and looks around, she is filled with emotion.

What do you think Linda was feeling? _____
_____

"George stood at the windows along the back wall of the living room, quietly looking out over the small backyard."

What do you think George was feeling? _____
_____

George's home consisted of many interesting items. Linda noticed the neglect in the upkeep of the place. She saw the evidence of a person who did not likely have the energy to take notice of his surroundings.

Have you ever been in a season like this, where even the idea of picking up the bathroom, making dinner, or taking a shower seems too heavy?

George's home in DC allowed Linda to see another layer, another glimpse of who George was. George lived his life well enough to work and keep a roof over his head. Based on what Linda sees, it is likely that at the end of each day, George simply had nothing left, no motivation to care for his home.

Linda saw beautiful artwork, messes, a mixture of life, and perhaps a mixture of loss of life, loss of care, loss of interest.

Isn't this just a perfect picture of most of our lives?

Lives filled with beauty, some we create ourselves, some given to us, like this beautiful home given to George by his parents. Lives filled with neglect, loss, mess, and pain.

It takes a special relationship, a feeling of solid trust to allow another person into one's home. Considering the state that George's home was in, George could have felt ashamed, embarrassed, maybe even regretful.

But Linda's quiet, thoughtful, and respectful presence helped him do what must be done to begin closing the door on this part of his life.

Do you have anyone in your life that you allow this close? Close enough to see the beauty and close enough to see the mess? Discuss below:

_____

_____

_____

_____

_____

Many people feel that they have to get themselves "cleaned up" before going to God.

They see Christians as "perfect people" and think there is no place for them in such a group. George did not clean anything up for Linda. He let her come in and as his eyes pooled with tears, he saw her supportive smile, and focused on the process of sorting through his stuff, closing the doors of this old home and in many ways, moving on to a new life, a new season.

Would it be possible that God is calling you to let Him in a bit closer? If He came into your heart, would you be fearful of what He would see? Would you hide the mess?

Listen closely friend. Pause. Be still. Hear this.

There is nothing in the home of your heart that would make God run from you.

There is nothing in your messes, your piles of neglect, your broken-down places, that God does not look at and say, "That is mine. This is where I belong. I want to be here with you, right here, right now. Let us do what needs to be done."

Guided prayer: *God, there are many things in my life that I treasure. There are things I hold so dear. Are they what is most important? I am not sure. Are You the treasure I have been seeking? I would like to show You my heart, invite You into my treasure trove and ask You to show me. What should I keep? What needs to go? Help me to make room for You. Help me not to be ashamed of what You see. Could it be that You want to make Your home in my heart? Am I holding things back from You? Speak to my heart, Lord. Thank You for being here.*

Chapters 29–34

The Gift of Love

In this next phase of events, there are more changes, more sacrifices to be made, more connections to have, more understanding of each other, more struggle and yet more joy in store for Linda, Bobby, and George.

In many ways this part of the book is when they truly become a family. And there are many moments where we learn more about love, **the gift of love**.

It seems that Bobby and Linda have given so much to George, but we know that they have also received much from George, so much love and opportunity to love.

How would you define what love looks like after coming this far in this story? **Circle your top three answers and explain them below…**

involves sacrifice	always feels good	can be difficult but worth it
comes easy and naturally	is welcoming and accepting	is a process that takes time
is always fun	can be painful	simply a feeling about getting your needs met
makes sense	is predictable and comfortable	

_____

_____

_____

_____

_____

"Why can't you take care of me during the day? George asked." George is told that he needs 24-7 care from his doctor and in his mind, the only person qualified for that job is Linda. She has been the one caring for him this whole time, so he asks her if he can hire her.

As usual, Linda goes to God and Bobby to get guidance and support. She says to God:

"Lord, is this the right thing to do? It would be so different. I don't even know what it would feel like to be home every single day instead of going to work."

How did Bobby respond? _____

_____

Do you think Linda could have done this without Bobby's support?

_____

_____

What does Linda decide to do? _____

_____

Would this be the kind of sacrifice you would be willing to make if you were in her shoes?

_____

_____

How did Linda feel about this change? _____

_____

Linda was peaceful and once again she prays for God's will and not her own.

"God, if this is not your will, please, please, stop me in my tracks. This is one of the most unexpected career decisions I've ever made."

When she told George the news that she would indeed leave her job and take care of him, George's smile spoke volumes. What a gift!

What do you think this meant to George to know that Linda would now be his full-time caretaker? _____

_____

Peta

Sometimes love can be more painful than we ever imagined, and yet loving another person even when it hurts can still be a gift. Sometimes love is not reciprocated. Sometimes love hurts. How do we reconcile these experiences in our hearts?

Think about your experience with love.

George and Linda visit his home again to continue sorting through his things. In chapter 32, Linda learns even more about George.

What was Linda's reaction when she saw his art studio? _____

_____

What painting was his favorite and why? _____

_____

How did George know Peta? _____

_____

How did George feel about Peta? _____

_____

What was the history behind Peta's story? Who was she? What was she experiencing in her home? _____

_____

_____

_____

_____

How did George describe Peta on page 137?

_____

_____

_____

_____

_____

It is hard to believe that Peta, such a loving and beautiful woman, would choose to stay with someone who mistreated her so horrifically.

What eventually happened to Peta? _____

_____

Once again, we find another layer of George's story unraveling. His pain was real, tangible, and raw. Peta was another loss that George lived through, but it seems barely survived. He still loved and missed her greatly.

Do you think George would have rather he never met Peta? Was there something George gained in loving Peta the way he did? _____

_____

Would you consider it a gift that George was able to love Peta?
Circle: *Yes   No*

Consider this: Perhaps George never would have gravitated so much toward Linda, if she had not reminded him of Peta.

In this sense, maybe we could even say that God used Peta to save his life. Thoughts? _____

_____

In **chapter 33**, George and Linda are sitting outside having a conversation. They did this often. In fact, it became part of the rhythm of their lives. Talking, eating, laughing, and simply enjoying each other's company. Their relationship is endearing and beautiful.

How could it be that two people could become so close?

It was clear that Linda knew how to love and that her love came from God, Bobby's unconditional love, her family, and children.

George had found love as a child in the eyes of his parents, yet as his father lost his mobility, there was a sense of shame in this relationship, a sense of guilt on George's part. George loved Peta and then lost her tragically. He loved his mother and lost her as well. And then he was alone for twelve years after his mother died.

George was likely extremely empty when he came to Bobby and Linda.

There were traces and memories of love, but it had been so long.

During this conversation on the porch, George teases Linda about Bobby getting jealous and Linda explains to him that she loves people, and he is "no exception."

Linda has a beautiful conversation with George about love on page 140. She seems to sense that perhaps George is afraid or concerned about loving Linda.

Maybe he is afraid to love again after all of his losses.

What stands out to you about this conversation? _____

_____
_____
_____
_____.

Why do you think it was so important for George to know that it was okay to love again? _____

_____.

Linda also begins to realize that she, herself, was learning more about love.

In this moment, she feels God's presence in the situation.

She says that "He decided to show His face."

Loving and being loved is a gift.

1 Corinthians 13:13 says, *"And now these three remain: faith, hope and love. But the greatest of these is love."*

Do you think that you have a good understanding of what love is? Think about what you have learned about love from Linda, Bobby, and George?

Take a look at 1 Corinthians 13 and write down all of the things that the Bible says "Love is..." Meditate on this and share your thoughts.

Love is_____

_____

_____

_____

_____

_____

_____

_____

_____

_____.

Chapters 35–40

Change

George's cottage was finally done, and Linda and George enjoyed the renovations together! George liked picking out what he liked, and Linda had a good eye for what looked nice.

They paid close attention to details such as what he would need to be comfortable, and they paid attention to what he would genuinely love, such as having more open space to look at the water.

Having someone take the time to help create a perfect space is really exciting and fun!

But actually, living in the cottage was not quite the fun experience George had imagined.

At first, Linda stayed with him, she gave him the attention she knew he needed, but eventually she had to go back to her home, her husband and her life...

How did George react to being in the cottage at night without Linda? _____
_____
_____
_____
_____.

How did George feel about the caretakers Linda hired to be with him? _____
_____

How did Linda react to George's response to the caretakers? _____

In many ways, George had become like a child for Linda. He needed her in such a sweet, innocent, and dependent way. He was attached to her and you can easily see why. But he also continued to process loss as he faced living in the cottage by himself.

In **chapter 36**, he recalls the loss of his mother.

One funny but amazing fact that George recalls is how his mother cooked breakfast for the two of them every morning, right up until she died. What an amazing mother he had! As he sat in his cottage, memories of her flooded his mind and heart.

What did George's mother enjoy watching him do? _____

George recalls the morning of her death. He remembers that there was no smell of breakfast in the air. When George's mother died, he was truly alone. She was the last person on this earth whom he had to love and be loved by. He recalled feeling like an orphan. This memory must have been very painful and traumatic as he stayed in the very house where this happened. Truly, this moment left a mark and now he was reliving it.

But George recognizes that something has changed!

He has been given the opportunity for love and family again. He realized he is not truly alone. Linda was still alive and loved him! He had Bobby and the kids and Linda's parents! He was part of a family again! The sweetness of this moment must have been almost too much to take in.

George recognizes this as a gift from God and his tears turn to tears of joy and thankfulness.

Isaiah 30:18 (NASB) says, *"Therefore, the Lord longs to be gracious to you, and therefore He waits on high to have compassion on you. For the Lord is a God of justice; How blessed are all those who long for Him."*

How does this verse speak of George's situation? How did the Lord show grace and compassion to George? _____

_____

_____

_____

_____.

George suffers and struggles as he realizes he has less and less control over his life. He greatly dislikes having caregivers come into his home. He wants to stay comfortable with Linda and this continues to create tension for him. Linda patiently supports him as he goes through this grieving process. God is with them and she knows it.

One day, Linda sees George walking across the lawn carrying a satchel! He tells Linda he is running away and coming back to live with her! What a sad but funny moment. George knew what he wanted and there was no going around it. He was going to let Linda know!

How would you feel if you were in George's shoes? Linda's shoes?

_____

_____

_____

_____

_____.

Ultimately, Linda continues to move forward, loving George as much as she can, hiring and replacing caregivers, making more memories with him, and trusting that God will provide.

Parties and puppies and boat rides, oh my!

What did Linda do for George's ninetieth birthday party? _____

_____

How did George feel about this party? _____

_____

Linda hoped so much to encourage George with his friends, with some fun and good food, but it did not end the way she planned, and this is just another lesson in love. George continued to buck the system! He did not want parties, new people, and new experiences. He just wanted his comfort, his family, Linda, Bobby, and his sweet memories. Linda and Bobby even tried to get him a puppy for comfort.

How did this turn out? _____
_____

Linda must have surely felt she had two strikes and was on her way to striking out in making George happy—but then came the boat ride. Love does not give up!
Describe the boat ride through George's eyes:

_____
_____
_____
_____
_____ .

There is a special moment when George looks at Linda and the water and the beautiful homes. *What does he say he would like to do?*

_____
_____ .

How does Linda see George on page 171? Write down the way she described him:

_____
_____
_____
_____
_____ .

This is one of the sweetest moments for Linda. Just seeing how happy George was in that moment was a gift. There was something so special that seemed to happen on that boat ride, as if George were able to simply be free. He had been struggling so much with the new caretakers and losing his independence and now this moment seemed to capture his soul.

Surrender

Fear is a strong motivator in most people's lives. Fear keeps people from opening up to others, taking risks, and accepting change; ultimately, the biggest fear involves letting go of control.

How would you say fear has played a part in your life? _____
_____
_____
_____
_____.

In this chapter, what is George holding onto? How would you describe what the rope represents? _____
_____
_____
_____
_____.

Why is he holding on? _____

What did he notice about the rope over time? How had it begun to change? _____
_____.

There was one strand left on the rope. What does God seem to be asking him to do about this last strand? _____
_____

You have been on a journey in this story. You have learned about God, about Jesus, the Bible, faith, obedience, trust… You have witnessed a beautiful story between Bobby, Linda and George.

Have you have been thinking about what this story, this message, could mean for you?

So let us rein things in for a moment here. Perhaps you are like George. You have a rope you hold onto, a sense of control over your life. You see that in time, in painful things, in hurt, in loss, your rope has been fraying and you cannot let go. Control is all you have left.

What would hold you back from letting yourself truly surrender to the God you have met in this story?

_____

_____

_____

_____

_____

_____

_____

_____

_____

How did George feel when He let go?
Warmth that was indescribable.

Comfort and peace like he had never felt before.

A peace so pure and so consuming that it was like being wrapped in an eternal hug.

Joy suffusing his entire being, so bright it made the sun seem dim.

Perfect peace and perfect joy.

Have you ever felt or experienced any of the above?
Circle: *Yes   No*

Write out your thoughts, perhaps a prayer…if you are ready, you can pray this one:

Lord, I am a sinner. I do not know You, but I want to. I am afraid to open up and surrender my life to You. You seem like an amazing God, but I do not know You yet. If Jesus died on the cross for my sins so that I could know You, then I accept Jesus into my heart. I want to surrender like George did. I want to live my life for you. I want to have a relationship with you like Linda had. I want to have faith like Bobby. I want to experience love like George. Help me to have this. Amen.

Chapter 42–46

A Time for Everything...

What did Linda begin noticing about George? How had he changed?

_____

_____

_____

_____

_____

Linda continues to enjoy her time with him. Their relationship is beyond special. Their bond is strong. They are learning from each other.

What does Linda learn from George? _____

_____

George tells Linda that he sees his mother at his cottage. Linda knows this is a sign that George is not only physically weakening, but perhaps mentally as well.

Not long after, George has another heart attack.

The doctors tell Linda there is nothing more they can do.

The doctors suggest keeping him at the hospital until it is time, but Linda refuses.

She keeps her promise to George that he will not die alone in a hospital.

She requests that he be brought home and propped up to see the view of the water.

Linda stayed with George throughout the remainder of his life. There was one thing she wanted to be sure of before he died. She asked him if he knew if he would be in heaven. She wanted to make sure he knew who Jesus was.

How did George respond? _____

_____

How did Linda feel about his response? _____

_____

One day, George tells Linda he sees "All the boys jumping off the pier."

She reflects on the joy he must be feeling to see his friends, "leaping into the water, carefree like children, just what Jesus said was necessary to enter the kingdom of heaven."

Matthew 18:3 says, *"And he said: 'Truly I tell you, unless you change and become like little children, you will never enter the kingdom of heaven.'"*

Why do you think you need childlike faith to enter the kingdom of heaven? _____

_____.

During George's last moments, he begins to watch Linda and do something. What does George do? _____

_____.

"At one point, he rubbed the top of her cheekbone so gently and with such love, deep in concentration."

How proud do you think George was of this final piece of art? What would it mean to Linda to be in this moment, watching George paint her portrait in the air with his finger?

_____

_____

_____

_____

_____.

In George's last moments, a pastor comes to speak to George and shares with him Psalm 23. Fill in the blanks of this most beloved Psalm:

"The LORD is my _____; I shall not want.

He makes me to lie down in _____ _____:
he leads me beside the still waters.

He _____ my soul: he _____ me in the paths of
_____ for his name's sake.

Even though I walk through the _____ of the shadow of
_____, I will fear no evil: for you are with me; your rod and
your staff they _____ me.

You prepare for me a _____ before me in the presence of
my enemies: you _____ my head with oil; my cup _____
over.

Surely _____ and _____ shall follow me
_____ the days of my life: and I will _____ in the house
of the LORD _____."

How did Bobby respond to this Psalm being read? _____

_____

What does this reveal to you about Bobby's feelings toward George?

_____

_____

What reassuring thing did the pastor say to Linda as George left this earth? _____

_____.

George was an army veteran and served in World War II. *Did you know this about George? Are you surprised?* Of course, George was full of surprises and knowing that he served his country just adds to the amazing person he was.

Linda placed several pictures of George and his family around the room at the funeral home. *Who did people say Peta looked like?*

_____

_____

What else did Linda learn about George from her children, Tara and Brandon? _____

_____.

Riches

How did this story end? _____

_____

Some would say the ending was the grand finale of it all! Some might say the ending is what made the story so amazing!

But that is not what Bobby, Linda and George would say about the ending of this story.

Surely, George's generosity in leaving all that he had, which was way more than anyone knew, blessed and touched the hearts of Bobby and Linda.

Sure, they were shocked and overwhelmed by such a generous gift!

Millions of dollars would cause most people to burst into tears with happiness and joy!

But the beauty of this story is that **the true wealth** was gained **way before** George's inheritance was left to Linda and Bobby.

What riches do you think Linda, Bobby, and George all gained through their time spent together?

_____

_____

_____

_____

_____

There is no amount of money that could equal the rich love that was shared between Bobby, Linda, and George.

And there is no amount of riches that could ever replace the love God has for you in Christ Jesus.

Now that you know their story, where does this leave you?

Romans 8:28 (The Voice) says: *"We are confident that God is able to orchestrate everything to work toward something good and beautiful when we love Him and accept His invitation to live according to His plan."*

We believe that God has a perfect plan for you, my friend.

You are loved.

You are cherished.

You may have found yourself in George's story. You may have seen yourself in Bobby's or Linda's.

May this next season of your life be spent seeking to know and love the God of the universe, and may your life become a portrait that displays the love of your heavenly Father for all to see.

About the Author

Liz Jones is a mother of two active, sports-loving boys. She has been married for eighteen years. Liz believes in the power of stories, especially the ones that speak of redemption, healing, and connection. She finds joy entering into creative work with people who love Jesus, and she craves authenticity. She is the women's ministry leader in her local church. Liz enjoys her career where she works with people with disabilities and assists them in finding meaningful work opportunities. Liz is always looking for opportunities to write. She has worked as a blogger, helped promote authors through book launches, and is now grateful to find herself as a new author doing what she loves: collaborating with other women, looking for God in real-life stories, and reaching out to people who are seeking meaning and truth.

CPSIA information can be obtained
at www.ICGtesting.com
Printed in the USA
BVHW040157120822
644441BV00003B/78

9 781638 145721